How

to

Be

Who

You Are

How to Be
Who
You Are

Rita Sherman

HarperSanFrancisco
A DIVISION OF HARPER COLLINS
PUBLISHERS

FIRST   EDITION

LIBRARY OF CONGRESS
CATALOGING · IN · PUBLICATION DATA

Sherman, Rita
    How to be who you are / Rita Sherman
        p.   cm.
    ISBN 0·06·251090·8 (pbk. : alk. paper)
    1. Self-actualization (Psychology) — Quotations,
maxims, etc. I. Title.
BF 637. S45 S19   1994   93·48282
170'. 44—dc 20   CIP
94 95 96 97 98   HCP—HK 10 9 8 7 6 5 4 3 2 1
This edition is printed on acid·free paper that
meets the American National Standards Institute
Z39.48 Standard.

Special thanks to Carole Abel, Lani A. Adler,
D. Lanier Young, Barbara Moulton, and the
Lisas, Bach and Schulz.

To the memory of
my dear Chester;
and to
Jeffrey Morton Seward,
who, thank God,
is very much alive.

Begin
with
gratitude.

Don't wait for conditions to be perfect to get going.

Don't get going just because conditions are perfect.

Do not expect to get out of overnight what it has taken a lifetime to get into.

Walk,
rather
than ride;
ride,
rather
than fly;
swim
whenever
you can.

Have courage sooner, rather than waiting for whatever requires it to come around again later.

Indulge your cravings for spinach.

Find your voice and use it.

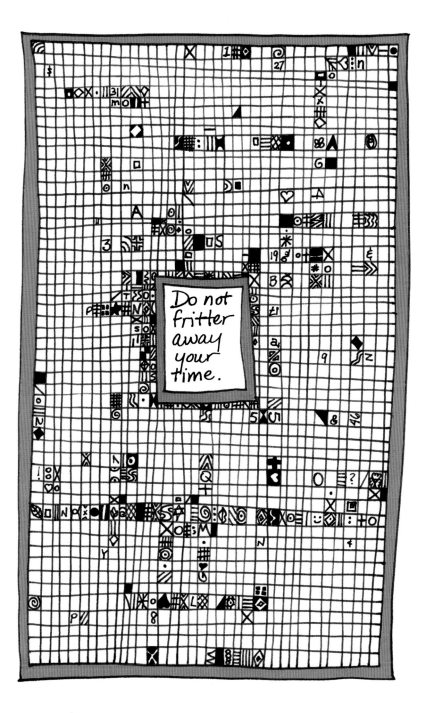

Value wisdom more than intelligence or wit, and kindness most of all.

Think of yourself as a porcelain bowl: strong, sturdy, purposeful.

Think of
yourself
as a
porcelain
bowl:
fragile,
receptive,
luminous.

Appreciate that the best way to get unstuck may be to stay stuck.

If you really must choose between being sincere and being polite, be polite.

Take
in
every
little
purr
that
comes
your
way.

Pay
attention
to
patterns.

Eat when you
are hungry;
drink when
you are dry;
do not do
either when
you are
neither.

Remember
that
you
yourself
are
your
life's
work.

Eschew most labor-saving devices.

eyes, // I all alone beweep my outcast state. But, you may say, we asked you to speak on what I do. For that's what it was. Orally. No, no go nor to Lethe, neither twist/Wolf's-bane tight,

• It is a truth universally acknowledged, that a single man is

• The Lord is my shepherd, I shall not want. Let us go then, you and I, when

• Fire over water; the image of the condition before transition. Leave back me, me/

• Now vee may perhaps to begin. Yes?

Read widely.

in want of a wife. When in disgrace with fortune and men's ... I got to do with a room of one's own?. No other word will ... wine somewhere I have never travelled, gladly beyond. ... Scott/The daughter of March has parsed, to the rare ... back. This urge wrestle, wrestling of day sticks.

that Aprille with his shoures ... inn and frozen — what has that ... rooted, for its poisonous ... somewhat my soul drew

When
everything
seems
impossible,
do the
acrostic
puzzle.

Ask yourself—
really ask
yourself—if,
were this day
your last,
you could say,
"there, that was
a good life."

Dear Taci and Donna: Elizabeth eats where she always has: in the living room, between the couch and the window. Gabriella eats in Chester's old spot, in the kitchen. I've put extra paper to make the places. If portable, I'd like Gabriella...

Gabriella, is in the...
the hall...

By wet is not available as have to just ask...

There are our nearby. Elizabeth is...
Gabriella is pretty...

...milk can, and of important. Dry food room, near the door in the bathroom.

We let her if she is too as just fed. If you in the hall. Also, please my dry kibble me!

...the table, and vitamins...
... on the bowl!

...about the bottle, or, if you can see,

When you
can't find
what you're
looking for;
stop looking.

If you are going to save for a rainy day, learn to recognize one.

Do not do something because it is expected of you.

Do not
not do
something
because
it is
expected
of you.

Know when
good enough
actually is
good enough.

When you can't find a single cat toy, clean.

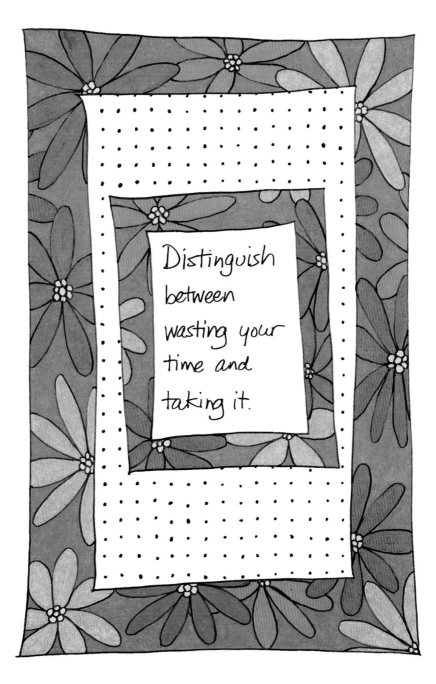

Distinguish between wasting your time and taking it.

Understand
that you
are always
alone.

Know
that you
are never
alone.

Live each and every day as if your life depended upon it.

Trust
the
process.

And
don't
forget
to
floss.